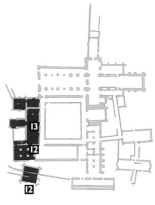

12 KITCHENS

At the far end of the refectory are the remnants of the
monks' 12th- and 14th-century kitchens. The earlier one,
attached to the west end of the refectory, has the rubble
bases of four massive pillars in the middle. The fire was lit
between the pillars, which carried a roof-vent overhead.
Food was handed into the refectory through a serving-hatch.
In the 12th century, in accordance with the Benedictine Rule
and Cluniac custom, the monks cooked in rotation, although
later on lay servants prepared the food. By the early
13th century, an obedientiary called the kitchener oversaw the
kitchen. In the next century, developments in the cooking,
presentation and serving of food led to the conversion of the
kitchen into a serving-room, above which an extra chamber
to the prior's lodging was later added. A new free-standing
kitchen was then built beside it, partly on a vaulted tunnel
over the stream. This too had a central hearth – surprisingly,
as by the 14th century most kitchens on this scale had
fireplaces against the walls.

13 WEST RANGE AND PRIOR'S LODGING

The buildings to the west of the cloister, incorporating the
remains of the priory's main storage cellar, the guesthouse
and the prior's lodging, have the most complicated structural
history of all parts of the priory, and are most easily

Above: Cluniac monks in their
refectory, from a 15th-century *Life* of
two early abbots of Cluny. Strict rules
governed the monks' behaviour
whilst eating, and, as in most other
areas of the monastery, talking was
not permitted

Overleaf: The prior's lodging viewed
from the south-west. Most
prominent is (to the left) the
14th-century prior's study (at
first-floor level) with one of its two
16th-century oriel windows. In the
centre is the early 16th-century
porch to the main entrance
to the cloister, and behind it
the late 12th-century porch which
it superseded

Left: An engraving of the early 1840s, showing the passageway through the 12th-century porch, facing its walled-up external archway. By this time the prior's lodging had become a farmhouse, and this room its dairy

understood with the aid of the reconstruction drawings that appear on the following pages. As laid out in the mid-12th century, the west range consisted of a long rectangle, similar in scale and detailing to the east range. The ground floor of its larger southern part, now open to the sky, served as a ready-use store for food and drink, managed by the cellarer, who was in charge of provisioning the priory. As in many monasteries, the main entrance to the cloister, used by the monks and for the arrival of goods, passed through the middle of this room – perhaps separated off by timber partitions. The original outer doorway can be seen under the later porch. Above the cellar was the guest hall, reached by an

12TH-CENTURY WEST RANGE

1 Main entrance to cloister
2 Food and drink store
3 Guest hall
4 External stair
5 Prior's private chamber
6 Outer parlour
7 Prior's chapel
8 Kitchen

Above: Adam, a 12th-century cellarer of St Albans, depicted in the late 14th century. The cellarer was responsible for the provision of the monastery's food and drink. He carries keys and a bag of money

LATE 12TH-CENTURY CHANGES
TO THE WEST RANGE

9 Two-storey porch with ornamental front

10 Room for privileged guests

11 Wells

external stair at its south end, where the priory's guests were fed and housed, a service that the Benedictine Rule required. Separated off at its northern end was a private bedroom for the prior – an arrangement not envisaged by the Rule but widespread after the early 12th century.

The northern end of the original block, still roofed today, contained the outer parlour at ground-floor level and the prior's chapel above. In the later 12th century a two-storey porch was placed in front of the original entrance, with a decorative outer arch, a vaulted passage behind, and a room above, perhaps for privileged guests. This porch was concealed when the existing outer porch was added in the 15th century.

14 Prior's Study

Further alterations to the west range followed in the mid-14th century, including the addition of a two-storey westward extension at its northern end. At ground-floor level was a vaulted room, perhaps intended as an office, linked in function to the room next door: this is the 12th-century barrel-vaulted outer parlour, accessible both from outside and from the cloister, where monastic officials could do business with laymen. In the corner is a spiral stair, originally leading to the prior's chapel and chamber, later to the first-floor room of the 14th-century addition – traditionally and plausibly called the prior's study – and now to all surviving upper rooms. The landing at the top looks out on the site of the chamber and guest hall, with the cellar below. When the study was added, its low-pitched roof, still partly in place, was extended over

First floor

Left: The main entrance to the cloister, passing through the west range. In the background is the original doorway of about 1140, and in front of it the arch and vault of the porch added in about 1180–90

the adjoining chapel, and the stone wall between them was replaced by a timber partition, both creating extra space and allowing the chapel to be viewed through it. A doorway in the north-west corner of the room led to a latrine. A fireplace was provided on the north wall, carried on a buttress and squinches on the outside, but was replaced in the early 16th century with the magnificent bay window, overlooking the approaches to the priory from the gatehouse. An 18th-century historian records that the window glass was richly painted

MID-14TH-CENTURY CHANGES TO THE WEST RANGE

12 Vaulted room
13 Prior's study
14 Latrine

Above: The elaborate canopied seat in the prior's chapel, added in about 1360

LATER 14TH-CENTURY CHANGES TO THE WEST RANGE

15 New chamber above prior's chamber

16 Two floors added to the porch

17 Walls creating courtyard and covered access to the hall

18 New chamber on site of 12th-century kitchen

19 New kitchen over stream

with heraldry (although even then partly 'broken and gone') and the letters 'J W joined by a knot', from which he identified it as the work of Prior John Winchelsea (1510–19).

After the suppression of the monasteries, the gables were once again raised to a steep pitch, the existing roof created above the 14th-century structure, the partition demolished, and the existing fireplaces – reused from elsewhere in the lodgings – inserted to provide two heated bedrooms. The two late-medieval wooden chests may come from the priory.

15 Prior's Chapel

The prior used the chapel for private prayer and to hear or say Mass, when not attending the church. As one of the most important interiors in the priory, it was much altered over the centuries, and the only surviving 12th-century features are the broad arch at the east end, which framed the altar, and traces of a geometric painting low down on its left-hand side. The east window was inserted in about 1300, and later in the same century the wonderfully elaborate canopied sedile, in which the prior or his chaplain sat at intervals during the Mass, was built into the wall to the right. Elaborate wall paintings, now difficult to make out, adorned the east end: these included (on the east window splays) early 14th-century representations of bishops and (on the right wall) an Adoration of the Magi, in which the figure of the Virgin is the best preserved. The two north windows, like those next door, were inserted in the 16th century, requiring the removal of two of the braces to the ceiling beams.

Later Alterations

Further alterations to the west range included, in the later 14th century, the creation of a new chamber over the earlier kitchen, and then, in about 1490, the existing outer porch (restored between 1929 and 1937). At the same time, walls were built on the west sides of the open spaces to either side of the extended porch, turning them into small courtyards. The final development was the construction of a first-floor covered passage or gallery running southwards from the prior's chamber, along the top of the courtyard wall, to the upper room of the outer porch (where the blocked door is still visible on the outside). It may have continued along the second courtyard wall to join the 14th-century chamber over the former kitchen. This gallery served as a private corridor between the most important chambers, bypassing the hall, but may also have been used for gentle indoor exercise, as were the 16th- and 17th-century 'long galleries' which developed from such structures.

First floor

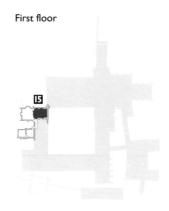

MONASTIC PRECINCT AND ITS BUILDINGS

The church and buildings around the cloister formed the nucleus of the monks' establishment, to which laymen were admitted only by permission of the guest master. Outside this, surrounding the north, east and west sides of the church lay an inner court, partly accessible to pilgrims and visitors on business. Enveloping the whole, and surrounded from the later Middle Ages by a high flint wall, was the 'precinct', estimated in 1734 at 40 acres, to which laymen (and women – if of high

LATE 15TH-CENTURY CHANGES TO THE WEST RANGE

20 Covered gallery and new porch

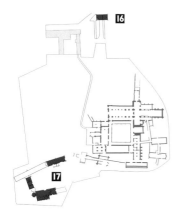

status, with permission or on special occasions) were more freely admitted. Many monks rarely left it.

16 GATEHOUSE

The main entrance to the precinct was through the gatehouse, now roofless but almost complete, which stands close to the present ticket office. Built in the early 16th century of brick and flint, this had a wide double doorway for horses and carts and a smaller doorway for pedestrians. Beside this was a small, well-lit room with a fireplace (separated from the passage by a timber screen), from which the porter controlled access to and from the precinct. Above was a large room, perhaps used as a court house.

17 BUILDINGS AND ACTIVITY IN THE PRECINCT

Gathered within the precinct were many buildings, resources and activities which sustained the daily life and economy of the priory, including fishponds, gardens, orchards, a vineyard, barns, a dovecote, a mill, granaries, the brewhouse, the bakery, dairy and stables. Traces of some of these survive within the eastern area of the precinct as mounds, ridges and hollows in the ground. The southern boundary of what may have been the vineyard can still be made out running due east of the ticket office, while further south, on the low-lying land by the river, are traces of fishponds. South-west of the main priory buildings, fragments of other structures survive, the nearest being those of a watermill for grinding corn. Beyond that, around three sides of a courtyard, are the remains of

Below: The gatehouse to the priory precinct. The scale and decoration of the building were designed to impress, and the coats of arms underline the priory's longstanding royal and aristocratic connections

1 Fitzalan arms
2 Royal arms
3 Warenne arms
4 Maltravers arms
5 Priory arms

buildings for processing grain – a kilnhouse for drying it, a barn for storing unthreshed sheaves, a granary and a malthouse and brewhouse for making beer – perhaps one of the best-preserved medieval complexes of its type. Until 1838 a large late-medieval barn stood near the gatehouse.

Above: Interior of the late-medieval priory barn, which stood within the precinct (near the present ticket office) until 1838. It was originally over 49m (160ft) and 11 bays long

CASTLE ACRE TOWN

From the priory the road to the town of Castle Acre skirts the outside of the medieval precinct wall as far as the small house called Abbey Cottage, at the corner with South Acre road. The cottage was identified in 1734 as a former chapel, perhaps on the basis of other information now lost, but this is certainly consistent with its large blocked east window. Exactly who would have used it is unknown. Ahead and to the right (south) is the impressive parish church of St James the Great, largely of the 15th century but incorporating earlier fabric. Beyond the western edge of the churchyard, a well-preserved stretch of the town's massive 12th-century earthwork defences can be seen through the hedge.

Further on lies the broad tree-lined Stocks Green. Today this is the main street, but it lies outside the northern rampart of the Norman town, and the houses to the south stand in its filled-in ditch. The town was entered by the late 12th-century Bailey Gate, from which Bailey Street – originally the main thoroughfare – leads downhill to where a second gate, now destroyed, passed through the southern rampart. Blocks of stone reused from the priory and castle can be seen in the walls of several houses.

Castle Tour

The best route to the castle is via a path off Bailey Street in the centre of the medieval town, which leads straight to the castle's west gate. This opens into the vast outer bailey, surrounded by earthwork ramparts. Looking down on this is the inner bailey, the result of successive alterations in the 12th century.

CASTLE ACRE CASTLE

Robbed over the centuries of most of its stonework, the most impressive remains of the castle are its gigantic earthworks. These define three main parts: at one end, rising round to the north, is the great mound of earth or 'motte', carrying the strongly defended inner bailey. To the south lies the far larger outer bailey. To the east a third, smaller enclosure (usually called the 'barbican'), reinforced an entrance facing open country. As such, Castle Acre Castle is a superb representative of the familiar 'motte-and-bailey' format, common both in pre-Conquest Normandy and Norman England.

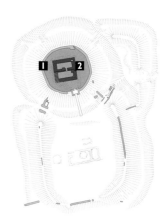

∎ INNER BAILEY

The earliest defences of the inner bailey, dating from the 1070s, consisted of a low bank carrying a palisade surrounded by a ditch: although the interior was raised by about 0.6m above natural ground level, the creation of a truly elevated motte was yet to come. A little later its original wooden gateway was replaced by a simple stone gate tower facing the outer bailey, with broad openings at front and back, both later made narrower. Probably there was a room above the entranceway, with a flat roof and battlements above.

❷ INNER BAILEY BUILDING

At or close to this time, a massive stone building was put up in the inner ward. As first built this consisted of a stone structure with walls averaging 2m thick, 24m square, and divided by a cross-wall on the longer axis. The southern room had an external south-facing door – later blocked, but still visible in the ankle-high remnants of the wall – and both rooms had a window at each end (both windows are now hidden). The building clearly had an upper storey, the northern walls of which partly survive, with a wooden floor. Part of a round-backed fireplace can be seen in the back wall, while the blocked embrasure of a window can be seen by looking over the railings to the west. The upper floor was probably reached by an external stair on the south side. Conceivably, a timber stair inside led to a further storey above. It had two large basement rooms and two above – one (and probably both) well-lit and equipped with fireplaces.

What was the Inner Bailey Building for?

It is less clear what this building was for. Was it an example of the familiar 'keep' or 'great tower' – a building designed for both defensive and residential use – or was it purely residential? The archaeologists who excavated the site in the 1970s felt it was the latter – a grand house – on the basis of its ground-floor entrance, large first-floor windows, and, crucially, the fact that its walls are significantly thinner than in

Above: The remains of the building in the inner bailey viewed from the south-east. In the foreground is the southern part of the original structure of c.1070, showing the alterations begun in c.1140 but subsequently abandoned. In the end, the alterations were confined to the northern part of the early building, shown in the background, which was converted into a great tower in c.1165

1 Junction between original external wall of c.1070 and internal thickening of c.1140

2 First-floor fireplace in the original building

3 Inner bailey rampart wall of c.1165

other great towers that had an unquestionable defensive function. In keeping with this, the excavators concluded that it had gabled ends rather than a continuous defensible parapet. On balance, this is the most likely interpretation, and is supported by the discovery in the 1980s of a similar thin-walled, double-pile late 11th-century building at Bletchingley, Surrey, and the existence of 12th-century buildings comparable in plan at Wolvesey Palace, Winchester, and (probably) at Thetford Priory.

Questions remain about its residential function. Did the Castle Acre structure form an entire house, with hall and chamber side by side in the same building? Certainly, such an arrangement could easily have been borrowed from the double-pile great towers which it closely resembles in plan. Or following the normal arrangement of grand houses at least in the following century, whereby 'great hall' and private chambers were housed in separate buildings, did it house the chambers associated with a long-vanished hall in the outer bailey? Only further research at other sites and further excavation at Castle Acre could provide the answer.

Inner Bailey and Building Transformed

Within about 70 years of its completion, William I de Warenne's building and the defences of the inner bailey were radically transformed. The rampart was heightened and crowned, for the first time, with a stone wall, part of which (to the east, complete with battlements) is now visible. Meanwhile, the ground level within was raised by 2.5m, and the walls of the house itself were massively thickened on the inside, blocking the ground-floor doorways and the windows

Left: The inner bailey defences and building as originally completed in c.1070, surrounded by the rampart in its earliest form, with wooden palisade, but with the addition of the stone gatehouse

Left: The inner bailey, showing the building undergoing the radical transformation begun in c.1140, intended to convert the building into a defensible great tower. In the left hand (northern) half the walls have been thickened up on the inside in readiness for adding further storeys above. To the south, the floor has been removed in preparation for the same operation. Meanwhile, the encircling rampart has been raised, partly burying the ground floor of the building, and crowned with a stone wall

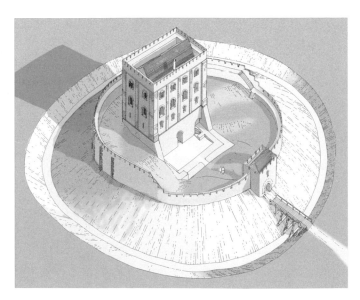

Left: The inner bailey and inner bailey building as they might have appeared by c.1165, following the completion of the scheme, but in reduced form, arrived at by converting only the northern half of the house into a great tower, and demolishing the rest (the footings of which are shown exposed for clarity). The northern half of the inner bailey wall was also heightened

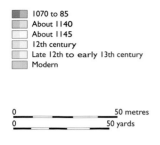

	1070 to 85
	About 1140
	About 1145
	12th century
	Late 12th to early 13th century
	Modern

0 ——————— 50 metres
0 ——————— 50 yards

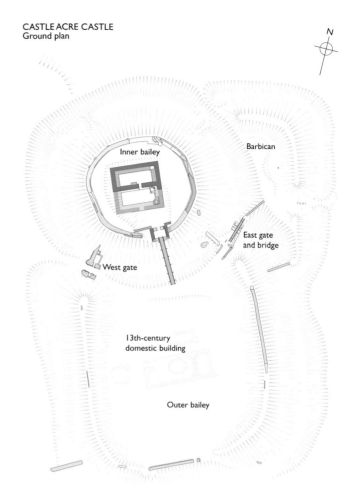

CASTLE ACRE CASTLE
Ground plan

N

Inner bailey

Barbican

East gate
and bridge

West gate

13th-century
domestic building

Outer bailey

Facing page: The castle seen from the south-east, overlooking the outer bailey with the inner bailey behind

at both levels. The joint between the original walls and the new work remains clearly visible. The intention, whatever the building's original purpose, was clearly to create a large and powerful great tower or keep, necessarily over 13m high if it was to overtop the rampart. But in the event a change of plan led instead to the demolition of the southern part of the partially converted building, and the strengthening and heightening of the remainder. At the same time, both the bank and the stone wall were once again substantially heightened. Whether the scaled-down tower was itself completed is unknown, but if so a height of at least 19m would have been required to command the heightened rampart.

The conversion as intended almost certainly dates from the 1139–53 civil war between King Stephen and his rival for the throne, Matilda, which encouraged the building and strengthening of castles all over the country. Archaeological evidence, suggesting a period of about or after 1140, points to the third earl William III de Warenne (1138–48) as the initiator. The change of plan in about 1165 – reducing the scale of the ostentatious tower but still strengthening the rampart – was perhaps made by the third earl's son-in-law and heir, Hamelin Plantagenet, a great castle-builder, but a man to whom Castle Acre was relatively unimportant.

Above: Early 18th-century engraving showing the inner bailey and its defences. The walls then survived in much better condition, complete with pilaster buttresses (left) and battlements (right). To the left are the remains of the west gate and to the right those of the east gate

Below: The west gate's remains viewed from the motte. To the right are the remnants of the two semi-circular turrets facing the approach from the town. In the foreground are the footings of the guard room

❸ OUTER BAILEY, ❹ BARBICAN AND ❺ GATES

The bailey forms an approximate rectangle covering 8,000sq m to the south of the motte, defended by massive earth banks with broad, deep ditches to the west and east, while to the south, where the rampart is lower, it was protected by the river Nar. As first built, the earthen rampart was less ambitious, and carried a wooden palisade. It was probably heightened along with the inner bailey after 1140, and then perhaps again, when it was crowned with a stone wall, part of which survives.

Linked to the inner bailey by a bridge, the outer bailey had three external entrances, the most important of which, to the west, remains the principal access from the town. This was approached across the moat – here since filled in – by a bridge, and defended by a massive stone gatehouse fronted by semi-circular turrets, the bases of which survive. Close similarities to the better-preserved Bailey Gate suggest that this was also an improvement of the late 12th or early 13th century. Behind, the vaulted passage was equipped with two sets of gates and a portcullis. To the north was a guardroom with a room above, beyond which the stone curtain wall continued upwards to join the inner bailey rampart.

On the east side of the bailey a second stone gatehouse, with a single pair of gates, faced the barbican. Linking the two was an impressive wooden bridge, later encased in a stone causeway, interrupted by a removable wooden section: the remains of both periods can be seen below the existing steel bridge, where modern timbers, marking the positions of the originals, project from the remnants of the masonry in which

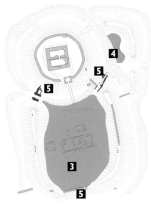

the originals were embedded. A third gate might have existed at the south end of the ward, opening onto a quay at the river's edge.

The practical buildings which every functioning castle required stood within the outer bailey — stables, storehouses and workshops. The castle probably enveloped the pre-Conquest parish church, although the church's exact site is unknown: later it was perhaps retained as the castle chapel. In the centre of the bailey a series of prominent ridges marks the outline of further buildings — probably a late 12th- or early 13th-century great hall, with an attached chamber at the east end and serving rooms and a detached kitchen at the other end. A third building to the north might have provided more private accommodation. More spacious, comfortable and easier of access, these buildings no doubt swiftly usurped the residential function of the inner bailey.

Left: The castle's west gate as depicted by the local clergyman, artist and antiquary Thomas Kerrich (1748–1828), in July 1782. The two turrets then survived almost intact, although the lower part of the facing had already been removed

History

Above: *Watercolour of the west front of the priory church in 1796, by Edward Dayes (1763–1804). The view was painted a decade or so before the site began to be tidied up for the benefit of visitors and in order to preserve the ruins. By 1804 the pigsty to the left, and the blocking of the main west door and the sheds within the nave, had been removed*

Castle Acre was the creation of the Warenne family, established in England by William de Warenne, a veteran of the battle of Hastings. William founded the castle, and his son and descendants founded the priory on its existing site, laid out the town, and improved them over successive centuries. By the late Middle Ages the castle had been abandoned, and in 1537 the priory was suppressed, shattering the local economy but ensuring that the essentials of 12th-century Castle Acre remain with us today.

THE WARENNE FAMILY, ACRE AND THEIR ENGLISH POSSESSIONS

In 1066, the year of William the Conqueror's triumph at Hastings, there was already a settlement at Acre, with a church and the principal house of a substantial landowner called Toki, possibly on the site of the future castle. Together with most of his class, Toki was dispossessed by the new regime, and his lands granted to a certain Frederick, brother of Gerbod, a Fleming whom the Conqueror had created first earl of Chester.

The Warennes took their name from the hamlet of Varenne on the Varenne river, near Dieppe in north-eastern Normandy. The first known member of the family, in the 1030s, is Ralph de Warenne, but the family's enrichment owed to his son William's military activity in support of William, duke of Normandy (later the Conqueror), in the mid-1050s. His reward included a place upstream on the Varenne called Bellencombre, already or soon after equipped with a massive motte-and-bailey castle. This remained the headquarters of the family in Normandy until 1204, and of its Norman branch until 1261. After 1066 William I de Warenne became one of the many continentals whose fortunes were transformed by the conquest of England – in this case aided, no doubt, by his

Below: The castle of Bellencombre, near Dieppe in Normandy, as shown on a map of 1813. This was the Warennes' principal base in Normandy. As at Castle Acre, it had a motte and a large bailey, and overlooked the town. The castle enclosed the parish church, as also at Castle Acre in the early Norman period

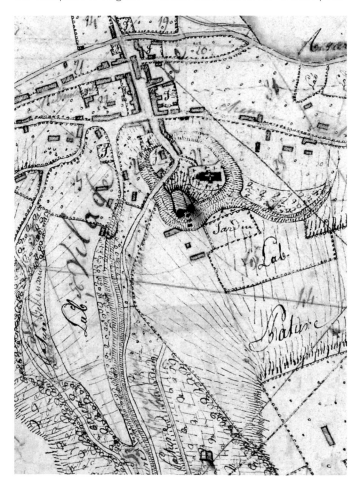

Above: Scene from the Bayeux Tapestry showing the Norman cavalry charge which opened the battle of Hastings in 1066. Among the horsemen present was William I de Warenne, one of the few named individuals whose participation is known for certain

Below: Conisbrough Castle (South Yorkshire), viewed from the south-west. The first castle here, as at Castle Acre, was built by William I de Warenne. The gigantic tower in the background was built for Hamelin Plantagenet, fifth earl of Surrey, in the late 12th century

presence at the battle of Hastings. Politically, too, he remained in the Conqueror's inner circle, being one of the four magnates appointed to govern in his absence in 1067.

By May 1070 Warenne had been given the 'rape' of Lewes, one of the swaths of southern England vulnerable to seaborne attack which the Conqueror entrusted to reliable magnates, and the Yorkshire manor of Conisbrough, where he built a castle. Warenne's first Norfolk possessions, however, were probably acquired not from the king but through his wife Gundrada, the sister and heir of Frederick, first earl of Chester, and it was probably by this route that he received his Acre property at some stage in 1070–1071. At about the same time he received further Norfolk holdings on the fall of Stigand, the disgraced archbishop of Canterbury, others after 1073 in exchange for land in Sussex, and still more after helping to suppress the revolt of Ralph of Gael, earl of East Anglia, in 1075. Warenne proved a successful manager of his property, and by the time of the Domesday survey of 1086, Castle Acre was not alone among his estates in being vastly more valuable than before the Conquest.

After the Conqueror's death in 1087, Warenne supported King William Rufus (1087–1100) against the old king's rebellious half-brothers, Odo of Bayeux and Robert of Mortain, and was rewarded with further property in Sussex and Surrey, including Reigate, and was created earl of Surrey. Now at the height of his career, Warenne was described by a near-contemporary as 'warlike, fierce in spirit, strong in body and distinguished in fame'. But in 1088 he was struck by an arrow while besieging Pevensey Castle (Sussex), held by Robert of Mortain, and was carried to Lewes, where he died shortly afterwards. He was buried in Lewes Priory.

CASTLE ACRE CASTLE AND PRIORY TO 1138

William I de Warenne's accumulation of Norfolk property would have encouraged him to establish a local power base by the early 1070s, and his choice of Acre was probably guided by its central position among his other holdings, its situation at the crossing of the Nar by Peddar's Way (the Roman road between north-west Norfolk and central East Anglia), and its long-established role as an estate centre. Archaeological evidence also hints that the castle was begun in this period, but in any case it was habitable in 1085, when Gundrada died there in childbirth on 27 May. As excavation has shown, the defences are of several periods, but the basic layout of two main earthwork enclosures was probably his. Castles such as William's were almost unknown in pre-Conquest England, but about 500 had been built by 1100. They played a decisive role both in achieving and consolidating the Norman Conquest. Capable of resisting a full-scale siege, they could delay or block an enemy's progress. Castles also acted as bases for controlling the surrounding country, administrative centres, high-status dwellings, sites for dispensing justice and entertaining, and permanent demonstrations of power. With these earthly advantages secured, William was soon, like so many Norman lords, to seek security in the after-life – and prestige in this one – through founding a monastery alongside his castle.

THE FOUNDATION OF THE PRIORY

The Warennes' first religious foundation in England, in the early 1080s, was the priory of St Pancras at Lewes. The monks came from the French abbey of Cluny, with which Gundrada's family already had connections, and which may also have favourably impressed them on an unplanned visit between 1081 and 1083. As a Cluniac monastery (probably England's first), its prior was subject to the abbot of Cluny, just as the prior of Castle Acre was to be to the prior of Lewes.

The initial gifts to the Cluniacs of property at Acre, consisting of the church of St Mary at Acre with its 30 acres of land and an additional 240 acres, were made between 1081 and 1085. Whether or not it was William de Warenne's initial intention to settle a group of his Lewes monks there, this had certainly happened by 1088, when he granted additional revenues to 'the church of St Mary … and the monks serving God there'. The early community probably numbered no more than three or four – as initially at Lewes – although possibly (as again at Lewes) further expansion may have been intended. Their church was almost certainly the parish church on its pre-Conquest site, but which, as is implied by a later source, had been enveloped within the castle bailey. The monks were probably provided with a small house beside it, and followed the daily Cluniac routine so far as their numbers, premises and other duties allowed.

Below: Late 18th-century engraving of the superb Tournai marble cover slab of Gundrada de Warenne's tomb at Lewes Priory, made in the 1140s in Flanders. The inscription, reproduced from her original tomb of 1085, alludes to her lineage, piety and lifelong mission to save the souls of her relatives. Rediscovered in c.1770, it is now displayed in the church at Southover, within the former Lewes precinct

William II de Warenne and the Refounding of the Priory

William I de Warenne's eldest son William, second earl of
Surrey (and the first to style himself earl of Warenne), had a
career as a soldier and politician on a par with his father's.
He took the side of Robert Curthose, brother of Henry I
(1100–35), when he invaded England in July 1101, which cost
Warenne his English estates. Rehabilitated, he took part
in Henry I's victory over Curthose at Tinchebrai in 1106.
Frequently in the king's company and celebrated for
his loyalty, he was rewarded with additional territories in
Normandy and Yorkshire. Warenne married Isabel de
Vermandois in 1118, soon after the death of her first husband,
Robert of Meulan. By then, however, according to a cryptic
reference in a 12th-century chronicle, she had already
been living with Warenne for some years, 'stolen by intrigue
and treachery'.

It was on William II's initiative, probably in 1090, that the
existing site was given to the monks, the existing buildings
begun, and additional endowments granted to support a
fully developed monastery. As one of his charters tells us,
he gave them: '… two orchards and all the ploughland from
the said orchards up to my castle in which … they have
founded their church, because that same place in which
they now live is too confined and highly unsuitable for
the dwelling of monks'. The grant thoughtfully included a serf,
'Ulmar the mason of Acre' to work on the new buildings.
Construction was a slow process, and the church was not
consecrated until 1146–8, and its west end completed only

The Cluniacs

Cluny, one of the most influential monasteries ever established, was founded in AD 910 in Burgundy by monks seeking a more rigorous interpretation of the sixth-century Rule of St Benedict, the basis of most medieval monastic life. In later years the Cluniacs were distinguished by the length and rigour of their worship in church, governed by minute systems of rules, and also by their love of art and decoration, as shown at Castle Acre. Cluny's example attracted many donations, and by 1100 there were about 700 monasteries which followed Cluniac custom, owed loose allegiance to the abbey and made it an annual payment. Other abbeys, meanwhile, were reformed under Cluniac instruction. Not being fully independent monasteries, they were called 'priories' – the 'prior' being an abbot's second-in-command.

Between 1076 and 1154, the support of kings and nobility encouraged the creation of over 30 Cluniac priories in England – ranging from fully developed houses such as Bermondsey (near London) to ones with just two or three monks. After about 1200, Cluniac houses became more formally bound together, and their heads were required to attend an annual 'chapter'. Meanwhile, by the mid-12th century Cluny itself had built what was the largest church in Europe until the 16th-century St Peter's in Rome. It was the third church on the site and mostly completed between 1088 and 1130. It was largely destroyed in the 19th century. Many monks from its scattered priories visited the church, and it was an inspiration to their benefactors and builders.

In later years the Cluniacs were distinguished by the length and rigour of their worship in church, but they also had a love of art and decoration, as shown at Castle Acre

Below: The abbey church at Cluny viewed from the north in 1617. Today little more remains of the church than the south transept and its tower (third from left)

Above: A late 14th-century image of Matilda, daughter of Henry I, whose struggles for the throne with her cousin King Stephen prompted the strengthening of many English castles, Castle Acre included. William III de Warenne fought against her on the king's side

Below right: King Louis VII of France leading the French forces on the Second Crusade, as depicted in the 14th century. William III de Warenne served in Louis's personal guard, but was killed before reaching the Holy Land

in the 1160s. The monks themselves probably moved to the new site in about 1100, once the east end of the church was finished, living in timber buildings while the rest of the priory was completed over the next 50 years.

CASTLE ACRE FROM THE MID-TWELFTH CENTURY

The second earl's son, another William, succeeded in 1138 while in Normandy, having deserted King Stephen (1135–54) during his attempt to take Normandy in 1137. After his return in 1139, however, he actively served the king in his long struggle with his cousin Matilda, Henry I's daughter, whose stronger claim had been rejected at her father's death in 1135 in favour of the male claimant. In 1146, swept up in the enthusiasm of the moment, he took the cross at Vézelay in France and joined the Second Crusade, but was killed serving in the personal guard of the French king, Louis VII, near Laodicea (modern Turkey) in 1148.

William III de Warenne gave further property to the priory at Castle Acre, and, it seems, embarked on a massive reinforcement of the castle. He was probably also responsible for replanning the town and building the massive ramparts which still partly surround it: certainly the mid-12th century is the generally accepted date for the similar arrangements at nearby New Buckenham and Castle Rising. At a time of uncertainty, the defences gave useful security, but also allowed tolls to be collected, a profitable concentration of commerce and manpower, and enhanced the visual impression of riches and authority already given by the castle and priory.

It was probably after the completion and occupation of the fortified town that the old parish church, within the castle,

0 ___ 150 metres

0 ___ 150 yards

N

Bailey gate

Castle

Castle Acre

Parish church

Chapel, now
a private house

Gatehouse

Line of town wall

Site of town gate

Shop, museum
and ticket sales

Precinct wall

Priory

Granary

Barn

Kilnhouse

Brewhouse

Line of medieval stream

River Nar

Site of fishponds?

Above: Plan of Castle Acre Priory, Castle and town

was replaced by a building on the site of the church of
St James the Great: certainly this had happened by about
1200, as the building is partly Norman. This would explain its
position outside the town – if by then fully occupied – and
the choice of dedication, both a Cluniac favourite and one
that distinguished it from the priory church of St Mary.

The Later Warennes and their Successors

At his death, the third earl's estates descended to his daughter
Isabel, and thus, together with the earldoms of Surrey and
Warenne, to her husband William of Blois, the youngest son
of King Stephen. The agreement of 1153 between Stephen and
Matilda that the king would be succeeded by Matilda's son
Henry Plantagenet, the future King Henry II (1154–89),
brought William exclusion from the line of succession, but he
was compensated with honours and lands, several of far
greater importance than Castle Acre. He died in 1159 on
campaign in France with Henry II. In 1164 Isabel then married
Hamelin Plantagenet, half-brother of Henry II, making him

Above: Impressions of the seal of John, seventh earl of Surrey and Warenne (1240–1304), from about 1250. The earl is shown here much as he might have appeared in combat – on a galloping horse, wearing a coat of mail and helmet. His horse wears a cloth 'caparison', bearing the 'checky' of the Warenne arms, as does his shield

Below: The exterior of the Bailey Gate, which guarded the north entrance to the fortified town. The slots for a portcullis and the positions of its two sets of gates can be seen in the passage

fifth earl of Surrey. Hamelin was a loyal supporter of the king in his struggles with his sons, and subsequently of Richard I 'the Lionheart' (1189–99).

At Castle Acre it was probably Hamelin who built the west gate to the castle and the Bailey Gate to the town, although, in the field of building, he is better known for his great keep at Conisbrough. His son, William Plantagenet, succeeded as the sixth earl in 1202, and although King John's (1199–1216) loss of Normandy to the French King Philip II in 1204 cost him his continental lands, he remained largely loyal to the king, as he did to John's son, Henry III (1216–72). Henry III visited Castle Acre at least four times, probably as the earl's guest.

William's son John, the seventh earl, succeeded in 1240, and in 1247 married the king's half-sister, Alicia de Lusignan, further reinforcing the family's longstanding royal connections. A significant statesman and soldier, John fought with the king on the losing side against the rebel barons under Simon de Montfort at Lewes (1264), and with him on the winning side at the battle of Evesham a year later. He went on to play a major part in Edward I's (1272–1307) wars with the Welsh and Scots, being defeated by William Wallace at Stirling Bridge in 1297. He died in 1304. How much use he made of Castle Acre is unclear, but he must have been there for at least some of Edward I's five visits between 1285 and January 1297. It was on the last of these visits to Castle Acre that the king received news of the clergy's refusal to pay tax without the pope's consent, initiating a significant political crisis.

John's heir, his grandson and namesake, earl of Surrey and the last earl of Warenne, did the family less credit. Under Edward II (1307–27) he played a risky game of switching alliances between the king and his enemies, although he was to be a steadier supporter of the next king, Edward III (1327–77). His personal affairs were dominated by his attempts to divorce his childless wife, the king's niece, and to provide for the children of his mistress, Matilda de Narford. Costly in other ways, his behaviour had a direct impact on Acre when in 1317 it was granted to Aymer de Valence, earl of Pembroke and ambassador to Rome, to encourage his advocacy for his divorce. Warenne eventually regained it, but it descended at his death in 1347 to his sister's son Richard Fitzalan, earl of Arundel, whose descendants retained it until 1558. By then, as indicated by a survey of 1397, the castle had long been derelict.

The Priory from the Twelfth Century to the Suppression

Following its relocation and enrichment by William II de Warenne, the priory had, meanwhile, continued to attract benefactions, including gifts from his descendants, the last of which was made by the sixth earl in 1315. By 1140, the priory held property in 28 parishes in Norfolk alone, and by 1291 in 50 more. This endowment provided most of its income, largely in the form of rents, tithes, gifts to the parish churches it controlled and related charges (such as for baptism and burial) and mills, in addition to the produce of its own home farm. All of this required time, effort and elaborate systems to manage and collect. Small gifts were also received from pilgrims 'peeping' at the supposed arm of the Apostle Philip, the priory's most important relic. Between 1115 and 1160 four priories were established, tied to Acre much as it was tied to Lewes, increasing its prestige and influence but also adding marginally to its resources. By 1534 its total income was calculated at £306 a year, placing it in the mid-range of English monasteries, whose incomes ranged from a few pounds to almost £3,500. The monks' greatest expenditure was on building (particularly in the 12th century), alms-giving, hospitality and the maintenance of up to 36 monks and a

Below: A monk distributes food to the poor and sick, a duty required by the Benedictine Rule. The drawing adorns a 14th-century manuscript of the Statutes of Pope Gregory IX, issued in 1231, reaffirming the Rule's authority

large number of servants. Extra costs sometimes pushed the priory into debt.

From the 13th century, periodic glimpses of the priory's internal affairs are offered by the 'visitations' of Cluniac officials, usually the priors of other houses, to report on the monks' finances and behaviour. In 1265, for example, the 32 brethren were found to be living with 'propriety and regularity', but were rebuked, among other things, for 'the habit of journeying and riding about the country, eating and drinking indifferently in the houses of laymen and secular persons'. In 1279 the 35 monks' conduct was satisfactory, although the prior was found, rather curiously, to be both extravagant and eager to resign.

Tensions also developed with Castle Acre's parent house at Lewes, largely because of its responsibility to Cluny for the Norfolk monks' behaviour and the appointment and conduct of their priors. Trouble erupted, for example, in 1283 when the earl of Surrey, backed by the monks, appointed his own candidate as prior, the 'contumacious, rebellious and disobedient' William of Shoreham. The prior of Lewes's attempt to impose his own candidate was met by armed resistance supported by the earl's men, the matter only being settled by the intervention of the abbot of Cluny himself. In the next century, another dubious prior, William de Warenne (half-brother of the equally wayward Earl John) absconded in disgrace, and is last heard of in 1351 as a 'vagabond' with a warrant out for his arrest.

Towards the end of the 13th century the priory also suffered, thanks to the threat and then the reality of war with France, when restrictions were placed on 'alien' monasteries

Right: Seal of John, earl of Surrey and Warenne (1304–47). The deer, swans, trees, birds and rabbits allude to the earl's many parks, known as 'garennes' in old French, and is thus also ('g' and 'w' being interchangeable), a play on his family name of Warenne

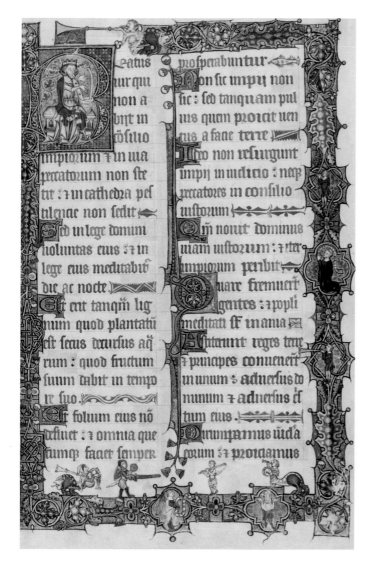

with French allegiances, even though the monks themselves were mostly English. Castle Acre was too far inland for the monks to be viewed as potential enemy agents, but by 1294 its community had shrunk, probably due to money troubles and the repatriation of French monks. The renewal of hostilities in 1324 prompted another government inventory of all 'alien' property, and Castle Acre was examined on 19 October that year. The original document only partly survives, but tells us that '18 gilded cups, valued at 3 shillings each' were found in the refectory, valuable silver vessels in the prior's hall, plenty of kitchen equipment and several horses in the prior's stable.

The response to these unwelcome attentions was to obtain English or 'denizen' status, achieved in 1325. Boosted by this, the priory in the later 14th century saw a revival of confidence, a number of improvements made to the buildings, and a recovery in the size of the community. As in many monasteries, the later Middle Ages saw further embellishment and alteration of the buildings, in response to fashion and increasing attention to comfort.

Right: Sketch map of Castle Acre town, Castle and Priory made in June 1734 by the Revd Francis Blomefield, initiator of Norfolk's first and most important county history. His highly observant plan and accompanying notes are a valuable source of information about buildings and other features now lost or changed

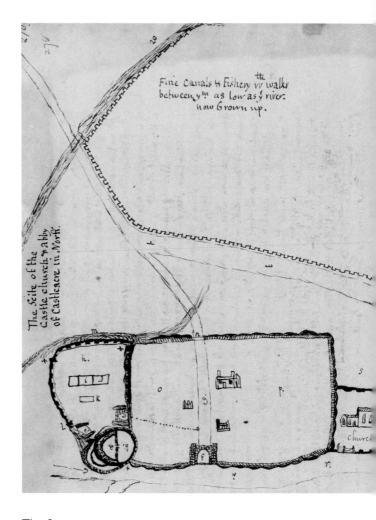

The Suppression

After almost 1,000 years of development, England's monasteries, then about 800 in number, were wiped out in the later 1530s by Henry VIII (1509–47): the motive – if under the cover of politics and ideology – was the seizure of their wealth. The social and economic consequences, good and bad, and since much disputed, were enormous: unquestionably catastrophic was the loss of so much of the country's medieval artistic and architectural heritage.

Ruthlessly and systematically managed by the king's chief minister, Thomas Cromwell, the process of suppression began in earnest in 1535 with an investigation of the monasteries' conduct. This was partly intended, if not openly, to build the case against them, however false, and the monks at Castle Acre were charged with a familiar catalogue of self-abuse, fornication and adultery. In the following year an Act of Parliament led to the immediate suppression of the smaller houses, and ultimately of the larger ones between 1537 and 1540. At Castle Acre the deed of surrender was signed on 22 November 1537 by the prior, Thomas Malling, and ten monks. They were probably granted small pensions and some, as was also usual, may have become parish or chantry priests.

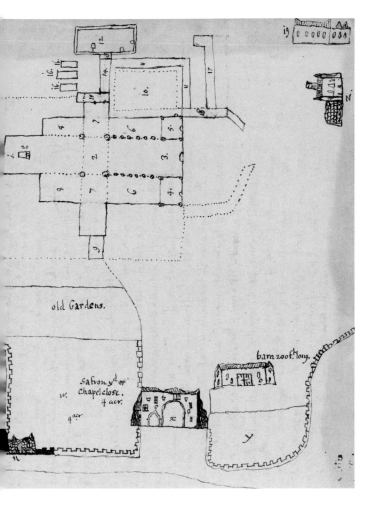

Castle and Priory from the Mid-Sixteenth Century

As previously arranged with Cromwell, John Howard, third duke of Norfolk, acquired the lease of the priory's site, lands and rights. Since then, both priory and castle have been in the same ownership. By the summer of 1558, the buildings were being demolished. Surprisingly, help was provided by the Cluniacs at Thetford – presumably in a futile bid for Howard's protection, but this also allowed them to secure St Philip's arm for their own church. The prior's lodging was retained as a house, in 1577 providing 'spacious and agreeable lodgings for one gentleman', and remaining in 'gentry' use well into the next century.

Sir Edward Coke and Castle Acre

In 1558, Thomas Howard, John's successor, sold both castle and priory to the London financier and diplomat Thomas Gresham, whose widow Anne sold them to Thomas Cecil, son of Queen Elizabeth I's lord high treasurer. In 1615 Cecil in turn sold the whole Castle Acre property to his brother-in-law, the outstanding lawyer and politician Sir Edward Coke (1551–1633), in whose family it remains. Interestingly, in an age when the deliberate preservation of obsolete buildings

Below: Sir Edward Coke, painted by Marcus Gheeraerts the Younger (1561–1636). Coke bought the priory and castle sites in 1615. Both still belong to his descendants

Above: The writer and philanthropist Hannah More (1745–1833), who visited the priory in 1777, painted in about 1780 by Frances Reynolds (1723–92)

Below: A ceramic tile from the priory, bearing the name of Thomas, a prior at Castle Acre Priory during the second half of the 14th century. It was found in a rubbish heap during excavations in 1972–83, although other examples survive throughout the priory. The text is in reverse because the mould was made the wrong way round

was virtually unknown, Coke paid immediate attention to the condition of the castle, ordering the 'finishing up of eleven battlements and other masons' work'. He was prompted, perhaps, by his well-attested historical interests, or by the prestige accrued to his not-so-ancient lineage by possession of what was, thanks to its battlements, visibly a medieval castle.

The Castle – Picturesque Ruins

From the 17th to the 20th century, however, the site was used for grazing and the masonry ruthlessly quarried for stone. Popular and antiquarian interest in the ruins for their own sake – ultimately to ensure their preservation – began in the 18th century, encouraged by the artistic and scholarly fashions of the time. A view of the castle was published in the 1730s, and it was visited in 1734 by the Norfolk historian Francis Blomefield, who found much of its 'lofty embattled wall' intact. Exploratory holes were dug in the late 18th century, and highly observant notes and drawings were made by Thomas Kerrich in 1782 (see page 31). Further investigations were made in the 1850s and the 1930s, but systematic study began – and has so far ended – with Jonathan Coad and Anthony Streeten's brilliant excavations of 1972–83. In 1971 Thomas William Edward Coke, fifth earl of Leicester, recognizing its historical importance, placed the monument in State guardianship.

Castle Acre Priory to the Present Day

Until the late 20th century, the more picturesque ruins of the priory attracted much more attention than the castle. The first visitor to leave a record was Matthew Dekker, staying locally. On 30 June 1728 he admired the 'old ruines of Cloysters and monastreys wh[ich] seem to have been very grand and Magnificent and were destroyed in Henry the 8ths Time' from across the river. Blomefield, in addition to making a detailed sketch plan of the town, castle and priory (see pages 44–5), 'sett 3 men to dig cross the Quire' to find the medieval floor. Public interest, at least of the leisured classes, was encouraged from the late 1730s by the publication of printed views, and in the second half of the century the site was attracting regular visits from the local gentry and their guests: one of them, the dramatist and philanthropist Hannah More, described Acre in 1777 as 'a very fine piece of ruins … not so large as Kenilworth, nor so beautiful as Tintern …' but possessed of 'a considerable share of magnificence, and no small portion of beauty'.

In August 1804 the artist John Sell Cotman (1782–1842) spent four days drawing at Castle Acre, noting recent damage to the ruins but also that Thomas William Coke (later second earl of Leicester) now intended 'to preserve them from

The First Custodian

William Savage became the first official custodian of Castle Acre Priory in 1929. His daughter Janet Boldero remembers:

'My father grew up in Castle Acre and went to the village school. I think he applied for the custodian's job because he was interested in church history. He had a wooden hut with a little coal-fired stove. It had a window that looked out to the top so that he didn't miss anyone coming in. Before the old brewery was excavated there were cowsheds and dairy buildings here. During the war, when they partly closed down the priory, he was taken on as a cowman. Then he worked as the postman. But at the weekends he came back, cutting a path through the overgrown grass and welcoming visitors. He couldn't leave it alone. It was a second home for us too. If we hadn't come down to help him we would never have seen him on a Sunday.

'He took great pride in his uniform and wore his medals on it. He was presented with the British Empire Medal outside the west front of the priory in 1951. The late Queen Mary used to visit when she was at Sandringham. One of her retinue once took her by the arm to help her get up the little winding staircase in the prior's lodging and she said, "Oh, no. My friend Savage will do it for me." And he was so thrilled by that. Some years ago an old gentleman knocked on my door. He came to tell me how grateful he was to my father for inspiring him when he was training to be a history master. It wasn't just a job, it was a lifetime's commitment. He worked here for 35 years and we held his memorial service in the priory church.'

'Queen Mary used to visit Castle Acre when she was at Sandringham. One of her retinue once took her by the arm to help her get up a staircase and she said, "Oh, no. My friend Savage will do it for me" '

Above: *The Prior's Lodging in about 1900, at an interesting moment in its transition from residence to displayed monument. The 17th-century rooms inserted between the block in the foreground and the porch have been removed, but the external stair to the prior's chapel is still in place. As the windows and garden show, the porch then still served as the custodian's house*

Below: *The porch as it is today, as restored by the Ministry of Works after 1929*

further dilapidation'. Within a few years, Coke's personal interest prompted active repairs, the removal of pigsties and other 'encumbrances', and further moves to stop stone-robbing. By 1843 there were enough visitors for the new tenant to be obliged to show them around, and their lavish picnics are described in the history of Castle Acre by the vicar, John Bloom, published in that year. The arrival of the railway at Lynn and Swaffham later in the decade boosted numbers still further, and no doubt encouraged the winding-up of the working farm in 1856 and the lease of the house to William Merritt, a gardener, to keep the place in order.

By the late 1880s, however, it was recognized that the site required an able-bodied full-time caretaker, and that he could be supported by a flat fee of sixpence per visitor. Meanwhile, the ruins had been excavated and studied by the pioneering historian and archaeologist William St John Hope, making them both easier to see and much better understood. The first (unofficial) guidebook, drawing on his discoveries, was published in 1908. In 1929, thanks to a suggestion by the Norfolk Archaeological Society, the main buildings were taken into State guardianship by the Ministry of Works. A new Custodian, William Savage, was appointed in 1929 (see page 47), and a massive programme of repair, the preparation of a new ground plan, and the publication of the first official guidebook swiftly followed. Since then, further conservation work and archaeological study has been accompanied by successive improvements to visitor facilities, the most recent including a new introductory display allowing historic images and artefacts from the priory to be viewed on site.